Ten Commandments For Wives

Benny B. Bristow

QUALITY PUBLICATIONS
P.O. BOX 1060
ABILENE, TEXAS 79604

ISBN: 0-89137-430-2

Table of Contents

Introduction

Almost every writer that chooses the home and marriage as his subject, mentions the sad fact that the home today is in trouble. Staggering divorce percentages are quoted to show that marriages in this nation are crumbling. Likewise, endless chapters are written in graphic details to explain why marriages are failing. These suggest such causes as, the modern day pressures of society, the working woman, the changed view of woman's role in today's world, the moral decay of this generation, and the list goes on and on! Now, who would deny that all of these, along with others, have brought pressures to bear; however, all of these things do not get to the bottom line. When a marriage fails, it is basically because either husband, wife, or both have broken some important commandments in marriage!

When God chose his nation Israel in the Old Testament, he sent them forth with Ten Commandments to lead them in their proper relationship to God and to one another. These "Thou shalt" and "Thou shalt nots" were to them very important, if they were to be successful. Their history reveals that all went well when they kept them, but failure, heartache, and even death came when they broke them.

Did you know that the same is true with marriage and the home? There are certain commandments, based on biblical principles, for husbands and wives, which, when broken, will destroy a marriage! Although the commandments given in this study apply to both husband and wife, they will be approached from the standpoint of the wife. However, after each commandment there is a list of discussion questions designed to help apply these commandments to husbands. It is also believed that when the wives think correctly about marriage, they will be able to help their husband be better husbands.

Many break these commandments without realizing such until the damage is done, and in some cases, one may be breaking only part of them. Therefore, whether your marriage is in trouble now, or whether you want to improve and sustain the good marriage you have, please study these commandments with a sincere, prayerful attitude.

I

Thou Shalt Consider Being A Wife Important

Chapter One

THOU SHALT CONSIDER BEING A WIFE IMPORTANT

Most little girls begin early dreaming of marriage and the home. They build their playhouses, arrange furniture, and cuddle their dolls. Their environment, and those by which they are influenced most day by day, suggest the fact that they will grow up, marry, and have a home. This becomes the most important dream of their lives.

The years pass and that "dreamed-about" day of the wedding arrives. Hour after hour of planning has been made with great joy and enthusiasm. During the wedding, the honeymoon, and for many months to come thereafter, she may feel that being a wife is very important. However, sooner or later the time will come when the newness of this experience becomes routine, and as the years come and go, there is a great danger that this woman will reach the decision that being a wife is not all that important. Sadly enough, this happens to some within months after the wedding. When this happens, all the relationships of that marriage will begin to suffer as happiness slowly disappears. This may happen to the wife, husband, or both, but in either case, this is a dangerous threat to a happy marriage, and will destroy everything unless help is received. To compound this problem, often a baby is born and more responsibility is added. Thus, it is so essential for a wife to have the right attitude toward being a wife.

When God set the principles and importance of marriage, He did not intend for such to be temporary. He wanted the happiness and joy of married life to be experienced throughout life. The ideal woman described in Proverbs 31, is a happy wife and mother. Not only did she consider her God-given role important, but her family honored her: "A wife of noble character who can find? She is worth far more than rubies. Her husband has full confidence in her and lacks nothing of value. She brings him good, not harm, all the days of her life. Her children arise and call her blessed; her husband also, and he praises her: many women do noble things, but you surpass them all" (Proverbs 31:10-12; 28-29).

Shakespeare wrote of the importance of a good wife in these

words: "Why man, she is mine own; and I as rich in having such a jewel, as twenty seas if all their sands were pearl, the water nectar, and the rocks pure gold."

It is at this point that many husbands fail. Very early a husband may be guilty of taking his wife for granted. He may leave the impression (sometimes simply by neglect and silence) that since he is earning the living, he is the important one. She simply stays around the house waiting for him. How wrong and cruel! One of his greatest blessings in life is to have a faithful wife at home. Therefore, he should make every effort to let her know. This can be done by telling her often that she is important, by sending occasional gifts and flowers, and by his attitude. Both husband and wife need to feel that their marriage, as well as their role as a husband or wife, is important.

The newness of being a wife will fade, but its importance should remain forever. Remember, if you consider being a wife unimportant, your husband will eventually be tempted to feel the same, but if such is important to you, and you continually give it your best, it will be important to him even if he fails in telling you.

Now, it is true that many things will happen along the way to suggest that being a wife is not important. For example, if you are spending all your time at home working as a faithful wife, some may make you feel that what you are doing is not important. Society may even suggest that the working woman (away from home) is the only one of importance, but don't you believe this! A faithful wife at home is second to none! This is not to say that a wife working away from home is not also important. In fact, obtaining a job to help the family may be her best way of being a good wife. However, when working away is not necessary, those who give their all at home are just as important, have a full time job, and may help hold the family together.

May we now look at some ways to help you feel that being a wife is important:

1. GIVE YOUR BEST AS A WIFE

Many wives do not feel important, because they are not doing their best. Not all wives are important — they are not seeking to be a good wife. We get out of life what we invest, and this is true in one's vocation, avocation, and religion. The person that spends his time at working trying to get by with the least effort possible will be a failure, and consequently, he will feel unimportant. Anyone that gives only a minimum amount of time and effort to religion will also feel religion unimportant! Likewise, the wife that shirks her responsibility to her home, children, and husband will lose respect for her role, but the wife that gives her best will recognize her importance. Can you imagine the ideal woman described in Proverbs 31, feeling unimportant?

2. REMEMBER, GOD CONSIDERS BEING A WIFE IMPORTANT

The society in which we live today often develops false concepts and standards about wives, but God and what is true, never change. The role of a wife is God's idea and all the modern technology and worldly thinking cannot change it. When you are the kind of wife that He specifies, be assured that you are VERY important. From creation, God made a wife to correct man's loneliness. He declared: "It is not good for the man to be alone. I will make a helper suitable for him" (Genesis 2:18). It seems from the context that both God and man were pleased with the first woman.

Solomon writes that prudent wives are from God: "Houses and wealth are inherited from parents but a prudent wife is from the Lord" (Proverbs 19:14). Just be the kind of wife that God wants you to be, and your importance will be felt.

3. HELP SUPPLEMENT THE INCOME AT HOME.

You don't have to be employed away from home to help your husband with the income. Neither does this mean that it is necessary for you to be employed to earn money at home. You can, however, supplement the income by the way you shop and prepare food. It has been said that a wasteful wife can throw more out the back door with a tablespoon than a husband can bring in the front door with a large shovel. On the other hand, a thrifty wife can plan special menus, prepare and store foods wisely, as she helps stretch the food budget. By giving her best in this effort, she is a co-worker with her husband with the income.

Therefore, I challenge you — never break this commandment! Instill deeply in the hearts of your children the importance of being a wife. Train their thoughts and your thoughts along with your hearts to feel that being a wife is IMPORTANT! Even if your husband, in his busy life of employment, fails to make you feel important, just keep believing that you are and keep living this truth, and sooner or later he will show true appreciation.

If you consider being a wife important, you will work harder to avoid breaking the other nine commandments, and the chances for you having a happy married life are great.

Remember: "A good wife is like the ivy which beautifies the building to which it clings, twining its tendrils more lovingly as time converts the ancient edifice into a ruin" (Johnson).

DISCUSSION QUESTIONS
THOU SHALT CONSIDER BEING
A WIFE IMPORTANT

1. Does family and society give little girls false dreams about their future marriage?

2. How does one deal with the "after shock" of marriage when the newness is gone?

3. To what extent does the right attitude toward the role of a wife in marriage help keep it important?

4. Discuss how today's society has harmed the true image of the importance of a wife.

5. What about the value of the ideal woman of Proverbs 31? Compare her to today's wife.

6. Compare the "working-away-from-home-wife" to the wife working at home.

7. Discuss why some wives are not important.

8. What place did God give the wife from creation?

9. How can a faithful wife at home supplement the husband's income?

10. How will the keeping of this commandment help in the keeping of the other nine?

HUSBANDS

1. How can a husband help keep the marriage from becoming routine?

2. In Proverbs 31:10-12; 28-29, discuss the husband's role in helping his wife feel important.

3. If husbands felt toward their wives as Shakespeare, in his quote, how would this help the wife's self-image?

4. Talk of the damage caused when a husband takes his wife for granted.

5. How are some of the ways that husbands can show appreciation as to the value of their wives?

6. Discuss husbands' attitudes toward wives working away from home.

7. How can husbands bring out the best in their wives?

8. Are husbands often guilty of wasting the income? How can he help the wife with economy?

9. Do husbands fail often in making their wives feel important?

10. Are most men concerned about being good husbands?

II

Thou Shalt Not
Let Courtship Die

Chapter Two

THOU SHALT NOT LET COURTSHIP DIE.

Most of you will agree that keeping this commandment is a big assignment. It is also a fact that the wife alone cannot accomplish this, for courtship is a team effort. However, it is also true that if the wife will do her part, the husband will more readily respond.

You can, no doubt, remember the days of your courtship. If all was as it should have been, you will recall joyful experiences as each of you was willing to make the other one feel very special. This young man was no doubt in command of your thoughts at every awakening moment. But after the "I Do" and honeymoon were over — after you felt that you had each other tied securely, did the courtship die?

Be assured that some of the courtship will die. Even though you might like to continue and keep all those warm, glowing, youthful feelings of courtship alive, such is not possible. However, the problem arises when the two of you allow ALL of it to die. When the children come, it is a temptation to pack away courtship, of any nature, along with youthful memories. Some wives feel that the children and their care, the preparation of meals, and housekeeping should be enough to make their husbands happy. The husband may make the mistake of believing that all of these things are enough attention for the wife! This is not true. As important as all of these things may be, they do not take the place of courtship. The question under consideration in this study is, "what can the wife do to keep courtship alive?" The following suggestions will help, if followed, and especially if the husband is instructed in regard to his responsibility.

1. Dress To Be Attractive.

Just think back for a moment to your days of pre-marital courtship. You probably did everything you could to be attractive to that man. Did you go all out for new dresses, ribbons in your hair, makeup, and just the right perfume? Did you want that favorite boyfriend to see you dressed sloppily, no make-up, and rollers in your hair? Did you ever say, "I would just die if he saw me this way!" Didn't you spend hours getting ready for his arrival? Why? Because you knew he would approve of your appearance, and you were right! Whether he mentioned it or not, he was thrilled at the appearance of such a beautiful package.

But what about after marriage? Too often this special concern for appearance is traded for sloppy house coats, bristled rollers, and a "don't care" attitude. Why do some wives act this way? Is it because they feel that after marriage, he no longer admires a beautiful woman? Remember, if a wife does not dress for her husband, he will see well dressed women at other places. Therefore, he may feel that his wife no longer cares.

The wife that takes her bath, dresses neatly along with jewelry and perfume, simply for the arrival of her husband coming home from work, may seem strange to some wives, but be assured that she is making an investment in happiness. After many other marriages have settled into a "don't care" attitude, and in some cases the problem of another woman, her marriage and courtship will still be alive.

What about at night time — is the way a wife dresses important? Chances are, that on the honeymoon she was decked out in beautiful gowns and negligees! But what about the following years of married life? Did her night apparel turn to comfort only without any concern for her husband?

Please be assured that home is the place to let your hair down as well as to roll it up. There are times when you want to be a "sloppy Jo" even in appearance. This is fine, and most husbands will not mind. The real problem arises when this becomes an EVERY "day and night" affair! A yearly dose of this will drive the idea of court-ship far from any husband's mind.

Be assured also, that courtship during marriage is not most husbands' strongest point. In fact, speaking as a man, we so often fall short. This however, should make the woman's role of attractive dress even more important. Perhaps she can help his weakness by the proper allurement.

2. Encourage His Wooing.

When a husband sees that his wife appreciates his wooing, he will happily pursue! As one writer put it: "With women worth being won, the softest lover ever best succeeds" (A. Hill). If the wife makes him feel that his advances for courtship are childish and foolish, he will stop soliciting her in love.

Surely there will be times when you don't feel in the mood for any type of courtship, and if the husband is worth his salt, he will understand and back away without feeling resentment. But this must be the exception and not the rule. If you encourage wooing on the basis of "few and far between", his desire for courtship will die. And be assured that such is difficult to resurrect!

3. Plan a Date

To the average married couple, dating ends when they both say the magic words, "I do". This is the way it happens, but this is not the way it should be. They may ask: "Since we eat and sleep together at home and go many places together, why go out on a date?" Thus, their whole lives fall into the pattern of work, home routine, church work, and rearing children without any special times alone. Why not plan a date? Encourage your husband to ask you (this is good communication, See Commandment No. 10) and then if at all possible, accept. When he decides to take you out to eat, to bowl, or to a movie, and you refuse him, showing no interest, he probably will not ask again. If you must turn him down, let him know that you would enjoy going and would he please ask again soon. The date does not have to be elaborate or expensive, the thing needful is to be together alone.

Can't you see that this second commandment is essential for a happy marriage? Resolve then, that you will do everything that you can as a wife to keep courtship alive and well in your marriage. Just do your part and encourage your husband to do the same, and a great reward will be achieved.

**THOU SHALT NOT LET
COURTSHIP DIE
DISCUSSION QUESTIONS**

1. Compare courtship before and after marriage.

2. Discuss to what degree a wife should dress up for her husband.

3. What problems can arise from a "don't care" attitude in the way a wife dresses during the day time?

4. What are your feelings about nighttime apparel?

5. What is your idea of romance in marriage?

6. Name some ways that a wife can encourage her husband's wooing.

7. How important is dating between husbands and wives?

8. Discuss ways a wife can encourage her husband to take her out on a date by good communication.

9. If you can't go on a date when he asks you, how should you handle this?

10. Is there a time when his advances and courtship are foolish? If yes, when?

11. If the husband fails in courtship, how can a wife help him?

12. Does a husband need more attention than cooking his meals, housekeeping, and caring for his children?

HUSBANDS

1. Are husbands as a whole, guilty of letting courtship die?

2. In what ways do they most often fail?

3. What happens when a husband feels that cooking, children, and housekeeping are enough attention for his wife?

4. How important is the husband's apparel? Cleanliness?

5. Discuss some of the ways husbands have the "don't care" attitude.

6. How important are flowers and gifts from the husbands after marriage?

7. Discuss the improper ways for husbands to give gifts.

8.   How should a husband react when the wife turns him down for a date?

9.   Where are some of the places that wives like to go with their husbands?

10.   What should husbands do to keep courtship alive?

III

Thou Shalt Not Make Thy Husband Feel Rejection

Chapter Three

THOU SHALT NOT MAKE THY HUSBAND FEEL REJECTION.

Perhaps the most depressing and hurtful feeling of the human heart is rejection. From the moment we are born, there seems to be a basic need of acceptance. The mother that cuddles that little bundle of joy, along with hours of baby talk and tender loving care, is meeting his need to be accepted. The real test, though, comes when he enters Kindergarten or first grade. He realizes fast that all people in the world do not accept him like mother and dad. He feels his first pangs of rejection when a classmate chooses someone else to be on his side in a game. After this, he may find a beautiful little girl which he claims for his girlfriend; however, rejection is felt when she has other ideas and chooses another. All these rejections in childhood may seem insignificant to adults, but to him, they are serious. In fact, they are each laying a foundation for the principle of later rejections.

After he grows up, marries, and is seeking happiness in life, his need for acceptance is still very critical. Since an important part of his life is centered around his wife, rejection from her can do extensive damage to him personally as well as damage to their marriage.

How does a husband react to rejection? The answer to this question will depend on his background (physically and spiritually). Notice some possible reactions:

I. He may become very depressed.

This reaction will spread itself beyond the marriage relationship to all other facets of his life. He may continue to function in all areas, but a certain amount of joy is missing.

II. He may back off from you as his wife.

He will feel estranged, and even during those times when you are showing complete interest in him, he will feel strong reservations. There will be an invisible wall between you.

III. He may turn to another woman.

This is especially true of men that are not Christians and even those that are Christians, in a moment of weakness, may get involved! Even if they are spiritually strong enough to refrain, they may turn to other women in their thoughts. Jesus warns: "But I tell you that anyone who looks at a woman lustfully has already committed adultery with her in his heart" (Matthew 5:28).

IV. He may lose self-respect.

There are so many things in life to pull him down. The environment where most men work is often called: "A dog eat dog world". When he feels rejection from those at work, he needs desperately to find acceptance at home. When this fails, it becomes a serious blow to his self-image.

Therefore, can't you see why that rejection on the part of either the husband, the wife, or both, is often at the root of a broken marriage? If you are convinced that rejection is a serious problem, perhaps you are ready to ask, "How can I avoid this?" There are no guarantees, but the following suggestions can help:

1. WORK TO KEEP HIM IMPORTANT TO THE FAMILY

A woman's life can be filled with so many important things that it becomes easy to set him aside. After all, he's a big strong man, he'll be alright! Thus, the children, shopping, hobbies, social appointments, telephone conversations, and even essential spiritual activities may crowd him out. Please note that I'm not suggesting that you must give these up, unless you have overloaded yourself beyond that which is reasonable! But what is being suggested, is that you take a look at your priorities. After God in your life, where is your husband?

The husband would be wrong in demanding all of your time and attention. If he loves you, he will even be understanding of all the activities in which you must be involved. However, he must feel that he is more important than all of these, and that you feel that he is!

2. SAY NO IN A KIND WAY.

No wife is expected to say "yes" to her husband's every demand.

In fact, there are times when it is best for him that she say "no". When this is absolutely necessary, learn to say "no" in a kind way. For example, he may decide to hold you, along with a few choice kisses, at your busiest moment of cooking a meal. It may be necessary, in this case, to say "no". There are two ways to do this, but one will destroy and the other will promote love. First of all, you can rudely pull away and say: "Can't you see I'm busy, doesn't your mind ever think of anything else?" The "no" will come through loud and clear, but so will the rejection. The second way you can say "no" is this: "Honey, I'd love to hold you, but at this moment I'm real busy. Could I please get to you later?" After this, if he continues, you might feel like being less kind, but if he has the proper love and respect, he will gladly understand. Let a very important warning be sounded here: Be sure you keep that promise! When you can, take a moment — give him your hugs and kisses and reward his understanding. If your promises to hold and kiss him later are not kept, they will eventually become another form of rejection.

3. BE INTERESTED IN HIS ACTIVITIES

A good husband will spend many hours working at home. He may be involved in such things as the yard, garden, flowers, shop, and special repairs. Take an interest in what he is doing. If he is working in the garden, go by occasionally and admire his work. If he has done a good job, mention this. If you enjoy this type of work, he would be delighted to have your help. There is a closeness obtained when you work and share things together. Your interest and acceptance of his interests make him feel accepted.

These three things may not seem all that important at times, but they are essential to keep your husband from feeling rejection. The area of sexual acceptance is also vitally important, but this is discussed in detail under Commandment number seven.

This is therefore, a commandment for wives that you will want to keep. Remember, the more you make him feel accepted, the more he will accept you.

DISCUSSION QUESTIONS
THOU SHALT NOT MAKE THY HUSBAND FEEL REJECTED

1. Discuss the background of husbands being rejected.

2. Why is rejection from a wife so damaging to a husband?

3. How can a wife help a depressed husband?

4. How does rejection from a wife tempt a husband in regard to another woman?

5. Should another woman become a problem, how can a wife deal with this?

6. Are most husbands "big strong men" when they are neglected by their wives?

7. Discuss how wives can keep from crowding out their husbands with a busy schedule.

8. How are the best ways to say "no" to your husband?

9. When you promise your husband hugs, kisses, and intimate consideration, how important is it to carry through?

10. Discuss the importance of doing things together.

HUSBANDS

1. Are husbands too sensitive in regard to rejection?

2. How can husbands deal with depression in the presence of their wives?

3. Discuss why turning to another woman is not a solution for rejection.

4. Why is it so important for husbands to find acceptance at home?

5. How do husbands reject their wives?

6. Discuss how a husband can keep his wife from feeling rejection.

7. In what ways are the three suggestions for wives in this chapter applicable to husbands?

8. Discuss how rejection from a husband can tempt a wife to think of another man.

9. Name some ways that husbands can make their wives feel more accepted.

10. Do you agree that rejection is often the foundation of broken marriages?

IV

Thou Shalt Not
Criticize

Thy Husband

Chapter Four

THOU SHALT NOT CRITICIZE THY HUSBAND.

There are many wives that would consider the keeping of this commandment impossible, while others might feel that the keeping of it is not necessary. Before you pass judgment on this commandment, please study some of the principles involved:

May we first understand what is meant by the word criticize. Webster defines criticize: "to examine or judge as a critic; censure:" Now, what husband wants to be censured by his wife? What husband enjoys looking upon his wife as his critic? Does this mean that a wife must close her eyes to his faults and failures? Does it mean that she even encourages him in his weaknesses? No! Certainly not! Eve is called Adam's "Helpmeet" (Genesis 2:18). This literally means: "Suitable help". How could a wife be "suitable help" to him if she refused to encourage his improvements?

Thus, the wife can help her husband in his shortcomings without harmful criticism. To accomplish this, there are some rules that should be observed:

1. RESPECT HIS HEADSHIP!

Wives across the land may ignore the fact, but God's word still says plainly that the husband is the head of the wife: "For the husband is the head of the wife as Christ is the head of the church, his body, of which he is the savior" (Ephesians 5:23). Again: "Now I want you to realize that the head of every man is Christ, and the head of the woman is man, and the head of Christ is God" (1 Corinthians 11:3). What does the husband's headship mean? It is compared to the headship of Christ, and what does that mean? Should the church criticize Christ as its head? Never! Since the husband is the head like Christ, shouldn't he be also respected as the head? Even though man cannot carry out the perfection of headship like Christ, such is still his model, and the wife must respect him in this

33

role. Any wife that helps her husband with his headship in mind, acts according to the will of God.

2. APPROACH ALWAYS WITH KINDNESS.

When a wife endeavors to help her husband, and to correct his weaknesses, she will deal in kindness. The attitude of kindness can go places and open doors where destructive criticism can never go. Some wives will lovingly and kindly correct a friend, and then make the mistake of rudely correcting her husband. Not only does this destroy a good husband and wife relationship, but it is certainly not a Christian attitude. The Apostle Paul writes: "Be kind and compassionate to one another, forgiving each other, just as in Christ God forgave you" (Ephesians 4:32). You may help lead your husband through kindness to improvement, but you can never, through rudeness, drive him anywhere except away from you!

Most husbands have built-in radars that pick up on kindness, and a little kindness will go a long way. If you truly respect him as your head, you will continually radiate kindness, and you will be rewarded with a successful love response. Try kindness, he'll like it!

3. IGNORE TRIVIAL MATTERS.

As you look back over your married life, how many times have you severely criticized your husband for things that were really unimportant? Some of these may have been simply escape valves used to let off steam from your other problems. These unimportant criticisms have a way of building up into serious damage to your husband and your marriage. Such can easily lead you to be a nagging wife. Solomon sounds this warning to all wives: "Better to live on a corner of the roof than share a house with a quarrelsome wife," "Better to live in a desert than with a quarrelsome and ill-tempered wife" (Proverbs 21:9,19).

Therefore, train yourself to ignore the little things. Do you ask, "how does one do this?" Just let love absorb them! Also remember, chances are, if he is the husband that he should be, he is ignoring trivial matters found in your life.

If it becomes necessary to mention some of these matters, why not approach such from a positive standpoint instead of the negative? If he is leaving his clothes in the floor, and most men will occasionally do so, instead of criticizing this weakness, why not say: "Honey, could I get you to help me with something?" After you suggest how he can help, if he agrees, express your appreciation with words, hugs, and kisses. This will go a long way in getting him to correct his problems.

4. LET LOVE BE YOUR GUIDE.

Did you know that all problems between husbands and wives, in regard to this Commandment, will be solved if you will let love be your guide? This means genuine love in all it facets, not a pretense or superficial love. When genuine love is your guide, all that you do, all that you say, and even your countenance will tell him that you are on his side. In fact, if there be love on the part of both husband and wife, you will respond to each other's needs. Remember, there is no limit to a man's response when he's responding to love.

Therefore, can't you see that you can be suitable help, a great influence in his life, and even be able to help him strengthen his weaknesses, without criticism? "DON'T CRITICIZE YOUR HUSBAND" is a commandment worthy of your keeping!

DISCUSSION QUESTIONS
THOU SHALT NOT CRITICIZE THY HUSBAND

1. Discuss the difference between constructive and destructive criticism.

2. Should a wife ever criticize her husband?

3. How does the wife respect the headship of her husband?

4. Discuss the difference between criticism and encouraging improvement.

5. How does kindness go a long way?

6. Talk about criticism and wrong motives.

7. What is a nagging wife?

8. What are the advantages of the positive approach over the negative approach in changing bad habits of your husband?

9. Discuss the wife as a "suitable helper" to her husband.

10. Why should love underline all your actions?

HUSBANDS

1. In what ways do husbands tempt wives to criticize their actions?

2. Do most husbands carry out their roles of headship?

3. How do most husbands rate as to kindness?

4. Is it true that husbands respond to kindness?

5. Do most husbands overreact to criticism from their wives?

6. Discuss husbands in regard to keeping clothes picked up and in place.

7. When a husband fails to show love, does this promote unkind criticism from his wife?

8. Discuss whether or not husbands nag.

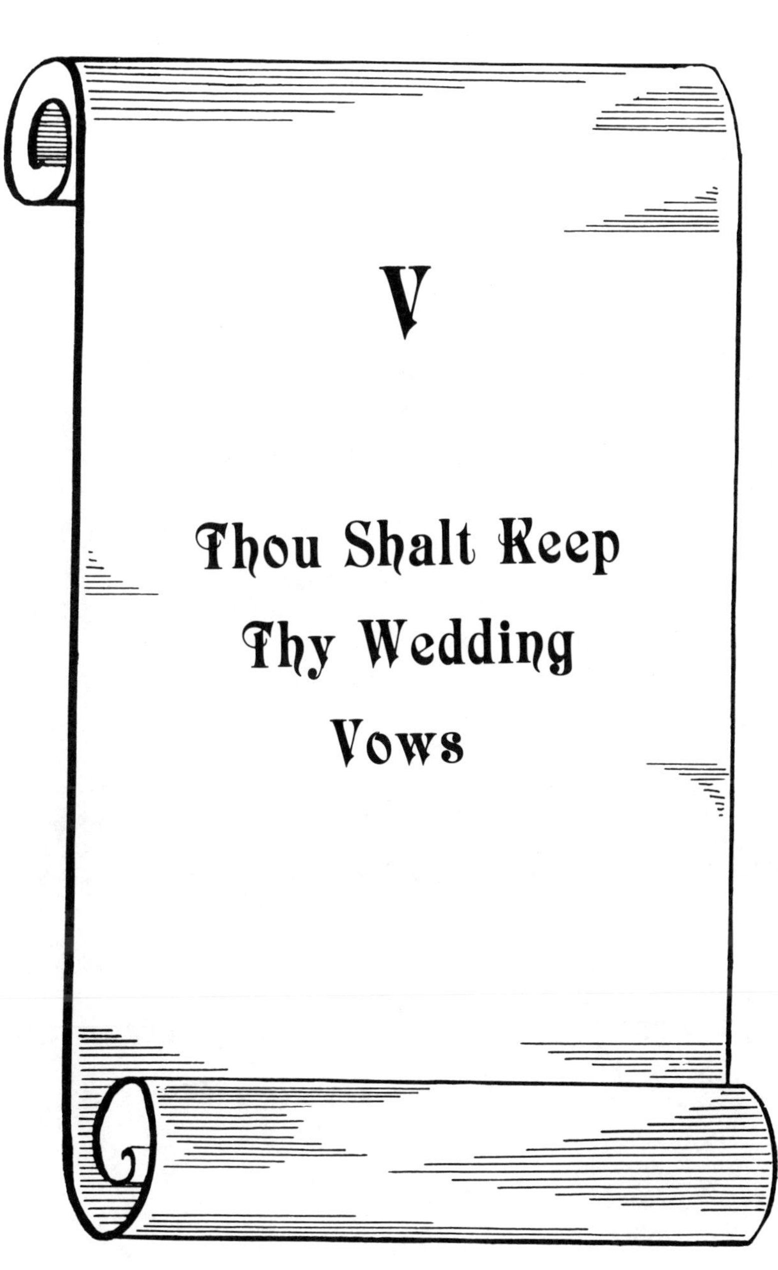

V

Thou Shalt Keep
Thy Wedding
Vows

Chapter Five

THOU SHALT KEEP THY WEDDING VOWS.

The most beautiful and memorable time in a girl's life is that time when she stands with her husband-to-be before the preacher, surrounded by a beautiful wedding party, to be joined in the holy estate of marriage. The ecstasy of this moment lights up her life with a brilliance never before seen in her life. After the prayer and several beautiful statements in regard to the sacredness of marriage, she (along with the groom) is called upon to take the marriage vows. These vows are in the form of promises to each other. One by one she hears them read as she waits for the last one. Then with all soberness she answers, "I do". In so many cases, she may not comprehend their meaning, but may observe only the general sound. One bride told me, "Please record the ceremony so I can hear it later, I won't hear a thing at the service."

Certainly, we can understand the excitement and stage fright of such a moment, but could it also be that we have not been taught the seriousness of the vows? Evidently not, because more lies are told at the altar than perhaps any other place! The majority that make these promises will not keep them! Approximately one out of three will turn their backs on all of them, while even a greater percent of the rest will ignore at least a part of them. Won't you agree that if the things promised in the vows were kept, the problem of divorce would be dissolved? Under this commandment, "Thou shalt keep thy wedding vows,"let us zoom in on what is generally promised.

1. WILT THOU TAKE THIS MAN TO BE THY WEDDED HUSBAND?

What does it mean to take a husband? Is this a casual responsibility of life? No, certainly not! It is one of the most serious assignments of life, but the majority do not take it seriously. The philosophy of the world says, "If things don't work out we can always get a divorce!" The Savior of the world says: "What therefore God hath joined together, let not man put asunder" (Matthew 19:6b). Thus, to the Christian, taking a husband is a permanent relationship and is very serious.

Taking a husband means that your life is now joined to another. Before this, you were a single individual and had to think only of what was right and best for yourself, but the oneness sought for in marriage involves two lives. As Jesus discussed a man leaving his father and mother to be united to his wife, he adds: "and the two will become one flesh. So they are no longer two, but one" (Matthew 19:5-6).

Since taking a husband involves becoming one with another, this means that you must now meet the needs of your husband. This is easier to do when the marriage is new, because the new bride gives most of her time to make her husband happy, but this may not be the case after the newness is gone. She may grow tired of his demands, and day by day begins neglecting him. It is at this point that she may regret marrying. The husband senses that things have changed as he begins to complain. Needless to say, bitterness, resentment, arguments, and even fighting become a part of such marriages. After this type of tension develops, she may neglect cooking his meals and especially refuse a sexual relationship.

2. TO LIVE TOGETHER AFTER GOD'S ORDINANCE.

This is a very important promise, but seldom kept. It is a promise to let God rule in your marriage as you keep His commandments. This part of the marriage vows is the rock foundation which will help keep a marriage alive and happy when other problems in life arise. A marriage that follows God's ordinance will have several things.

First of all, both husband and wife will be a Christian. This will bring to the marriage such things as honesty, forgiveness, patience, and moral purity. These characteristics will help purify the relationship, and believe me when I tell you that all marriages are tested! Problems and pressures will arise, but with God's way of life on your side, you can overcome them.

In the second place, following God's ordinance in your marriage will lead you to seek the true meaning of love. The spiritually involved will go deeper into the concept of love than does the world. In fact, the unselfish Agape love so beautifully portrayed in the New Testament will rule their actions. Just take a look at some of the active principles which will be in marriages with agape love: Based on 1 Corinthians 13, love is very patient, very kind; love knows no jealousy; love makes no parade, gives itself no airs, is never rude, never selfish, never irritated, never resentful. Love is never glad when others go wrong. Love is gladdened by goodness, always slow to expose, always eager to believe the best, always hopeful, always patient; love never disappears.

Those that are living together after God's ordinance as Christians will have the open line of prayer between themselves and God. As difficulties and pressures arise between them, they can call upon the help of God. Prayer will not only help them keep humility, but will also tap help from the strongest source of power in existence. A marriage that is in contact with the throne of God, can survive the many storms of life.

3. WILT THOU LOVE, HONOR, TRUST, AND SERVE HIM IN SICKNESS AND IN HEALTH?

Most couples assume that all will be smooth sailing in their marriage. Like most story book endings, they plan to live happily ever after. However, this does not represent true life. Chances are that there will be sickness as well as health. It may be in the form of injury, diseases of the body, or even mental illness, but any of these can bring pressures to bear on a marriage. It may be easy to love, honor, trust, and serve in health, but the real test comes in sickness. If there be the true oneness which God commands in marriage, true and faithful service will come. The wife or husband will serve the other during these trying moments as if it were their own bodies. The apostle Paul introduces this idea to the church at Ephesus. He is writing about husbands loving their wives and says: "He who loves his wife loves himself. After all, no one ever hated his own body, but he feeds and cares for it, just as Christ does the church" (Ephesians 5:28-29). This same principle applies to wives. When we become personally ill, we give ourselves undivided attention. We choose the foods that will help our illness, as we serve ourselves with tender attention. Now, Paul's argument is this, since you are one flesh with your mate and must love your mate as yourself, you will care for your mate in the same way you would care for yourself! Therefore, the serving him in sickness is a God-given principle. This may be difficult to do, especially over a long period of time, but if there be agape love – one will serve.

4. BE TRUE AND LOYAL TO HIM, AS LONG AS YE BOTH SHALL LIVE?

What a forceful promise! You don't promise to be true and loyal until the going gets rough or until the new wears off, or until he gets older and makes changes, or until you find another, but as long as ye both shall live! When God set up marriage from the beginning, He made no arrangements for divorce. He gave this iron clad rule: "Therefore what God has joined together, let man not separate" (Matthew 19:6). Later Moses permitted divorce because their hearts were hard. Jesus adds: "But it was not this way from the beginning." Then Jesus gives his teaching: "I tell you that anyone who divorces his wife, except for marital unfaithfulness, and marries another woman commits adultery" (Matthew 19:8-9).

Marriage then, is a permanent contract. When a husband or wife promises loyalty as long as they shall live, God expects them to keep this promise. Again, can you imagine the millions that have lied to God at the marriage altar?

Every Christian married couple should review the vows they took often, and then give their best to keep them. Parents should teach their children the awesomeness and sacredness of the marriage vows while setting the proper example by keeping their own. Truly, there will be a genuine blessing to all that work to keep their wedding vows.

DISCUSSION QUESTIONS
THOU SHALT KEEP THY WEDDING VOWS

1. Discuss how that "I do" so often becomes a lie.

2. How can the sacredness of the marriage vows be taught to our children?

3. Marriage is a permanent relationship. How does this generation consider it? Why?

4. Why is being a Christian so important to a happy marriage?

5. Discuss how agape love is essential to a marriage that lasts.

6. How does prayer help in marriage?

7. What pressures are brought to bear when injury and disease of the body come upon couples?

8. How does Paul's statement: "He who loves his wife loves himself" apply?

9. How does God feel about divorce?

10. Discuss the one exception given in Matthew 19:8-9.

11. Should adultery make a divorce compulsory?

12. Is a wife compelled to forgive adultery?

HUSBANDS

1. Are the marriage vows important to most husbands?

2. Discuss the importance of teaching boys the importance of the marriage vows.

3. Who promotes and causes divorce the most, men or women?

4. What is involved in the words: "Leave" and "cleave" in Genesis 2:24?

5. In many marriages, husbands are not Christians. How does this affect such marriages?

6. How do most husbands cope with the poor health of their wives — well or poorly?

7. Discuss husbands loving their wives as themselves.

8. In our modern age, is adultery mostly a husband problem?

9. How should a husband handle the unfaithfulness of his wife?

VI

Thou Shalt Not
Fail in Loving
Thy Husband

Chapter Six

THOU SHALT NOT FAIL IN LOVING THY HUSBAND.

There has been more written and said about love than perhaps any other subject, and yet, there is still misunderstanding. It is a common thing to hear the words, "I'm in love", but how short lived are these words in too many cases. Why is this so? Because the word love is used with a meaning that stops on the surface. The word love is applied to all walks of life without showing any difference in its meaning. A woman may use the same word whether she is expressing her feelings for her husband, her dog, or apple pie. Love needs to be viewed with all its different levels in mind!

Perhaps it will help us understand the word love more completely, by observing three words used in the Greek language. These three words translated love are: Eros, Philia, and Agape. Eros means a sexual type of love, Philia is a tender love of friendship, and Agape is a love which unselfishly considers the needs of the one loved. Each one of these has its place in love between husbands and wives. However, many marriages begin mostly with physical attraction, Eros love. Sexual attraction between husbands and wives is important, but this alone will not last unless it is reinforced by friendship and unselfish concern.

How does a wife possess the love of friendship and unselfish service? Just how are these two important types of love, along with sexual attraction, obtained? The answer to these questions is found in understanding the Greek word for love, Agape. Let us observe some concepts of Agape as they apply to love between husbands and wives:

1. LOVE MUST BE INITIATED.

Most of our lives we have heard the expression, "falling in love", which leaves the impression that love strikes as lightning without any effort on our part. Now, physical attraction may come upon us

suddenly, but the kind of love that is around when all the fireworks
are over must be initiated. For example, Paul commands:
"Husbands, love your wives" (Ephesians 5:25a). To Titus he gave in-
struction for older women to: "train the younger women to love their
husbands" (Titus 2:36). Thus, love must be initiated.

In Ephesians 5:22,25, wives are told to SUBMIT, and husbands
are told to LOVE. Perhaps you are ready to say that most husbands
do not initiate love, and you are right. This could possibly be man's
greatest weakness. Classes need to be taught to husbands, and
books read on how to love their wives. It is also a fact that many
wives refuse to submit because husbands fail to love.

What can you as a wife do, if your husband fails to initiate love?
Should you become angry, refuse to submit to him, and punish him?
Yes, if you don't mind destroying your marriage and happiness! On
the other hand, if you want to be his help meet (suitable help) you
will initiate love, while encouraging him to do the same. You see,
Agape love loves those that are not loveable! When you become
angry, refusing to function as a good wife, you may destroy him, but
Agape love will seek the best for the one loved. Thus, if you initiate
love and work patiently and lovingly to improve his ability to love,
you will help him as well as yourself.

2. SEEKS THE GOOD OF THE ONE LOVED.

All of you are familiar with John 3:16, "For God so loved the world
that he gave his only begotten son...." Here is Agape love in action!
God did not love the world because the world was loveable – not
because the world deserved his love, it was because God had the
world's best interest in view. Because of God's love, millions, down
through the centuries, have loved God, and have worshipped and
honored Him, but before all of this, He loved.

There are a few exceptions, but as a general rule, the wife or husband that loves for the happiness of their mate, will find happiness
themselves. The wife that initiates love, even if her husband fails in
his God-given assignment, will (most of the time) win his love. Give
love and it will be returned, is a great principle to follow.

3. IT'S A GOD-GIVEN COMMAND.

We often speak of loving our husbands or wives as something that
is optional. To the person of the world, this is true, but to the Christian, it is a God-given command! The word does not say: "Husbands,

love your wives if you so choose." Or "teach the younger wives to love their husbands, if they wish to", but a direct command is given. There are those that will teach all day the importance of obeying commandments in regard to faith, repentance, and baptism, but feel no conscience pangs when they disregard the commandment to love their husband or wife. All commandments are important, and not just the ones we single out.

4. IT IS A COMMANDMENT THAT WE DO.

Millions love their mates only if they feel like it. This may be fine for the ways of the world, but it is not the Agape love of a Christian. The mother that has a new baby gets up in the wee hours of the night to care for his needs. Why does she do this? Is it because she feels like it? No! She may be so sleepy and tired that she is ill, and yet she does it! Why? Because she has a love that seeks the good of her baby. Remember, 1 Corinthians 13, doesn't tell you how to FEEL love, but how to ACT in regard to the one loved. (See Commandment Number 8).

By now you should be able to see that Agape love removes selfishness from our lives. It will cause you wives to set aside your personal feelings for the good of your husbands, and, believe me, it will cause him to love and respect you.

Agape love can be illustrated by the short story of the man that was very poor. At Christmas time he wanted to purchase combs for his love who had beautiful long hair. To accomplish this, he sold his gold watch. His love was also without money, but she wanted to purchase a gold chain for his watch. Therefore, she sold her hair and purchased the chain. Imagine what it was like when they exchanged gifts! She had no long hair for the combs, and he had no watch for the new chain. Do you suppose they were disappointed? No, they both received the greatest gift of all – LOVE!

Don't ever forget that the ingredient which holds a marriage together is love.

DISCUSSION QUESTIONS
THOU SHALT NOT FAIL IN LOVING THY HUSBAND

1. Discuss the importance of love being viewed at all levels.

2. Discuss the three Greek words and their importance in the husband-wife relationship.

3. Is there love at first sight? What type?

4. Does the Bible make love between husbands and wives optional?

5. How does a wife submit to her husband?

6. Discuss what to do if a husband fails to initiate love.

7. Apply Agape love to marriage.

8. Is the command to love in marriage as essential as the commands of repentance and baptism?

9. Should a wife initiate love only if she feels like it?

10. The Bible tells us how to act in regard to love instead of feel; what is the difference?

11. Discuss how the short story about the combs and watch chain teach an unselfish love.

HUSBANDS

1. At what level of love are husbands usually weakest?

2. Discuss what is involved in the command: "Husbands, love your wives."

3. How do the statements, "husbands love", and "wives submit" go together?

4. Why are many husbands weak in loving their wives?

5. What kind of classes would help husbands to initiate the proper love for wives?

6. Do you feel that as a whole, husbands are willing to sacrifice for the cause of love?

7. Are husbands more selfish than wives?

8. Do you agree that love is the ingredient that holds marriages together? If yes, discuss your reasons.

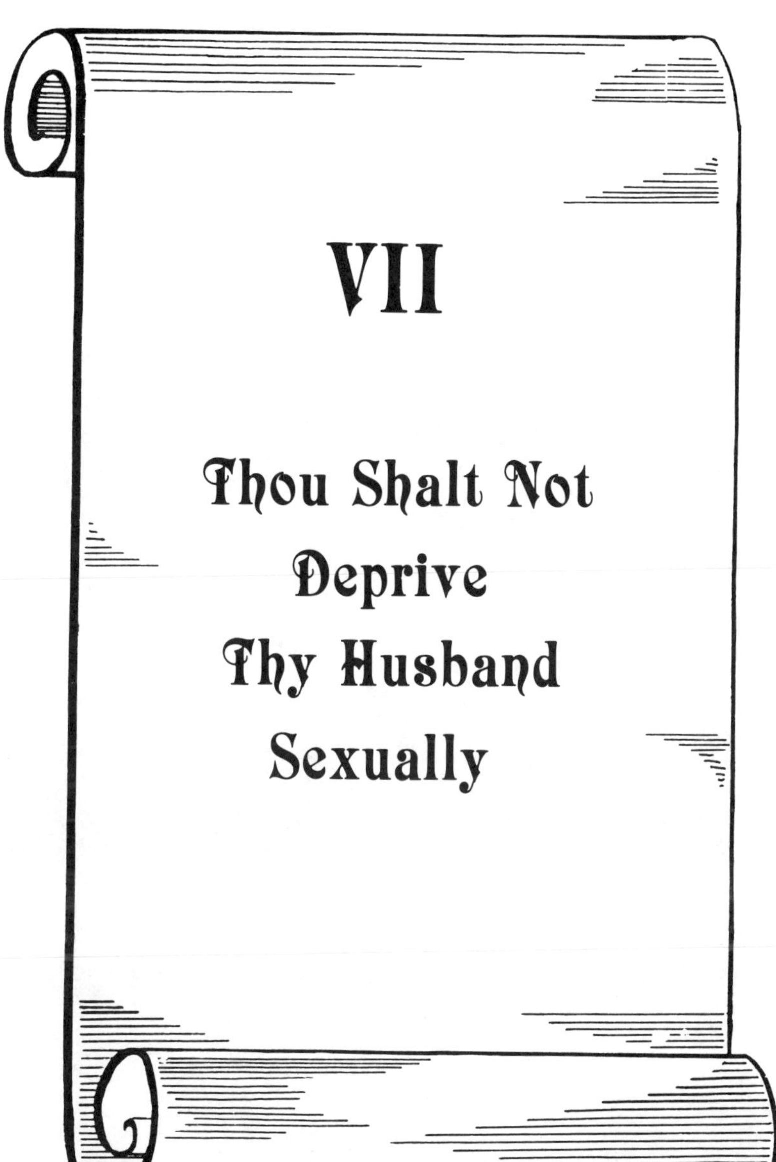

VII

Thou Shalt Not
Deprive
Thy Husband
Sexually

Chapter Seven

THOU SHALT NOT DEPRIVE THY HUSBAND SEXUALLY.

This seventh commandment is based on Paul's writing to the Christians at Corinth: "The husband should fulfill his marital duty to his wife, and likewise the wife to her husband. The wife's body does not belong to her alone but also to her husband. In the same way, the husband's body does not belong to him alone but also to his wife. DO NOT DEPRIVE each other except by mutual consent and for a time, so that you may devote yourselves to prayer. Then come together again so that Satan will not tempt you because of your lack of self-control" (1 Corinthians 7:3-5).

Paul's teaching could not be made any plainer than this, and yet millions have never accepted it. Why is this true? Note the following reasons:

> 1. The sexual relationship is a very intimate relationship, therefore very little teaching in the past has been done. "Just let nature take her course", has been too often the attitude.

> 2. Millions have grown up with a warped view on the subject. Since the sexual act between those not married is condemned in the Bible as the sin of fornication or adultery, too often guilt is felt even when the relationship is between husband and wife.

> 3. Many husbands and wives do not feel that they are "one flesh." It seems that they want to be single while married. Even though Paul says that each one's body does not belong to themselves alone, most do not accept this.

When we finally learn to accept God's teaching on the subject of sex between husband and wives, things will be improved. Mankind has distorted the beauty of sex in almost every way possible, but God keeps the subject pure, beautiful, and in its proper place. (See

Background Material – "Sex and the Bible")

May we turn our attention now to some guidelines which will help wives avoid depriving their husbands sexually:

1. CONSIDER THE SEXUAL RELATIONSHIP IMPORTANT.

Both the Bible and authorities in secular research declare that this union between husbands and wives is very important. Those who do not feel that such is important often say: "Sex is not everything" or "there is more to marriage than sex". This is certainly true, but it is also true that marriages crumble every day because of failures in sexual relationships. The sexual union between a man and a woman where love is present, is the foundation on which all other facets of marriage is built. Companionship, being a cook, a bread winner, and a babysitter can be obtained by hiring such services. Two people might even live together and share these responsibilities, but such would not be true marriage without the sexual union.

Please note something else – sex between a man and a woman is not limited to just the sexual act. Even the things done together, regardless of how small, have sexual feelings. For example, there is a difference between a man and a woman having a cup of coffee together than two men or two women! God made men and women sexual beings, and there is no way that such can be completely ignored. Yes, a couple may reduce their relationship down to merely a partnership, just living together to share responsibilities, but this is not marriage the way God designed it.

Remember also, that this union does not begin and end with the sexual act itself, for God intended that this union bring a couple together to the point of being one flesh. When a husband and wife discontinue this sexual relationship, they will feel far away from each other even though they continue to sleep in the same bed. If you wish to lose closeness with your husband, if you desire to revert back to a single life while still married, then consider the sexual relationship of no importance, and such will happen! This land is full of men and women who decided that this part of marriage was not important, and now they have a broken marriage. God made such important from the beginning, and anyone who decides otherwise will find rejection and disappointment.

2. RECOGNIZE THE DIFFERENCE BETWEEN MAN AND WOMAN IN THIS RELATIONSHIP.

Very early in life children discover that boys are made physically different from girls, but the real difference, as to sexual feelings and special needs, are often never discovered. When the husband fails to understand his wife, and the wife fails to understand her husband, there can be serious problems. There are, of course, many things between man and woman that are similar, but the ones that are different often produce problems. Would you please consider some of these differences:

3. MEN ARE MORE VISUALLY STIMULATED SEXUALLY THAN WOMEN.

This is a fact of life that God made in man and needs to be recognized. This means that your appearance can enhance your relationship. Since women are not as visually stimulated as men, they may not understand them at times. Your husband may not understand why you are not like him in this regard. In fact, when you don't visually respond to him, he may feel that he is not appealing to you. However, when husbands and wives understand this difference, each can work harder to reassure the other.

4. HUSBANDS REQUIRE LESS PREPARATION FOR SEXUAL UNION THAN WIVES.

This is a place in marriage where good communication is very important. Remind him of this fact and request that he not rush you in this important phase of the relationship. Encourage him to patiently lead you to the point where you will welcome a sexual union with him. At the same time, the wife should not prolong the union too long for his sake. Again, in a close marriage, good communication will help both husband and wife to be considerate. When the proper kind of love is present, each will seek to make the other happy.

5. MEN HAVE A SEMINAL FLUID BUILD-UP IN THEIR BODIES WHICH HEIGHTENS THEIR DESIRE.

When a husband goes a week or more without a release of seminal fluid, his sexual desire for his wife, especially if she is physically able to respond to his needs, is stronger. If she continually refuses him, he may even experience some physical pain as well as mental distress. The wife does not have this, and can usually go longer without a strong desire. Thus, the wife should understand this difference between herself and her husband so that his needs can be met. The longer such needs are neglected, the more he will be tempted to have lustful thoughts, and in some cases, if not a strong faithful Christian, may seek a relationship outside the marriage.

This principle must have been in Paul's mind when he wrote: "to avoid fornication, let every man have his own wife, and let every woman have her own husband" (1 Corinthians 7:2). Again: "Do not deprive each other except by mutual consent – so that Satan will not tempt you because of your lack of self-control" (1 Corinthians 7:5).

6. MEN DO NOT WISH TO BE THE ONLY INITIATOR OF SEX.

It is true that God has made the husband the head of the wife and his role often requires him to take the lead. Generally this is true in the marriage relationship, but occasionally she should be the initiator. By the wife having this option, she can let him become aware of her needs as a woman. Also, it is a way of re-assuring him of her love and desire for him. Paul did not stop when he said: "The wife's body does not belong to her alone but also to her husband." He continued, "In the same way the husband's body does not belong to him alone but also to his wife" (1 Corinthians 7:4). Paul is saying, in regard to the husband's body, the wife has her rights.

7. YOU ALONE CAN MEET HIS NEEDS.

The third guideline is also very important. The man you are married to, or will marry, has many needs. He will need food, housekeeping, companionship, and close friendship, and all of these needs will be met by a faithful wife. But, please remember, should you neglect any of these, he can obtain such from others. He could eat at a restaurant, rent a furnished room with maid service, and find close friendship with another. However, there is one area, if your husband be a faithful Christian, where he CANNOT seek fulfillment for his needs from others, and this is in the sexual union. Should he do so, it would be adultery! Therefore, if you do not meet his sexual needs, he will be deprived of this important part of his life.

There may be occasions, due to illness, when it is impossible to meet his sexual needs, and the husband that loves his wife even as Christ also loved the church and gave himself for it" (Ephesians 5:25), will understand. But, if he is deprived because of your lack of love, selfishness, or long extended grudges, he will feel pain and rejection.

As this God-given relationship grows, and as you become truly one with your husband, both of your lives will reflect such. Even your children and friends will see by your actions that you are happy. Remember, the best sex education for children is to see hugs, kisses, and the daily touching of mom and dad who are happily married.

This commandment number seven is so important if you are to have a happy well adjusted relationship in your marriage. Why not do your best to keep it?

DISCUSSION QUESTIONS
THOU SHALT NOT DEPRIVE THY HUSBAND
SEXUALLY

1. Why has such little teaching been done in the past on the sexual relationship?

2. What are the dangers behind: "Just let nature take her course"?

3. Discuss how the Bible distinguishes between sexual relationships that are sinful and acceptable.

4. Where does the truth lie between the extremes that "sex is essential" and "sex is not everything"?

5. In what ways is the sexual union with love the foundation for all other facets of marriage?

6. Name some things that are sexual in nature other than the sexual union.

7. What does the concept of "one flesh" mean to you?

8. Discuss some of the problems that can arise between husbands and wives because men are more visually stimulated sexually than women.

9. How can wives help their husbands to realize that they need more time to become ready for the sexual union?

10. To what degree is a wife responsible to help her husband "avoid fornication?"

11. How do you feel about wives occasionally initiating sex?

12. Discuss why meeting the husband's sexual needs is more impoortant than all other physical needs.

13. How do parents teach sex education to their children?

HUSBANDS

1. Do you feel that husbands are too demanding in sex? Do they place too much emphasis on it?

2. In what areas do husbands need the most improvement in regard to their sexual relations?

3. What attitudes can most husbands improve upon in regard to the sexual union?

4. Do most husbands recognize their wives' sexual needs?

5. Are husbands selfish when it comes to the sexual part of their marriage?

6.   To what degree are you in sympathy with the seminal fluid build-up causing a heightened desire?

7.   Name some weaknesses husbands may have in their role of initiators of sex.

8.   Do husbands or wives really believe that their bodies belong to the other as Paul says in 1 Corinthians 7:4?

9.   If husbands are deprived of sexual union by their wives, does this give them the right to have an affair?

10. Should adultery occur by a deprived husband, is the wife guilty of sin also?

VIII

Thou Shalt Seek
An Ideal
Marriage

Chapter Eight

THOU SHALT SEEK AN IDEAL MARRIAGE.

Life can hold many happy and thrilling moments, and one of these moments is when two people, deeply in love, are united in marriage. Even though there may be tears on such occasions, they are tears of joy. It is a time of radiance, laughter, and hope; a time when plans are made, dreams are born, and the future looks the brightest.

Even with all this happiness and planning, not all who are married will live happily ever after! It is impossible to write of the heartache, pain, unhappiness, and tears that come from marriages that fail! What causes these marriages to fail? Is it because the idea of marriage will not work? No, the fault lies in man and woman failing to build an ideal marriage based on God-given love. When love is absent, all commandments relating to marriage are broken.

God intended that all true marriages be totally entwined together with love: "Husbands, love your wives, even as Christ also loved the church, and gave himself for it" (Ephesians 5:25). In like manner, wives are to be in subjection and love their husbands (Ephesians 5:22; Titus 2:4). But what is this all-important ingredient called love? Why is it so important? There have been many beautiful sounding definitions for love, but they generally fall short of its total concept. Love, as the Bible presents it, can be recognized only by what it does or does not do. Love is an action word, and this is the way the apostle Paul presents it in 1 Corinthians 13. Love is demonstrated. It is known by its results.

An ideal marriage does not happen by chance. It must be diligently sought after by both parties. Marriage and the home are from God and have brought happiness to millions throughout centuries of time, but only when these God-given principles of love have been observed.

1. LOVE IS PATIENT AND KIND.

The marriages that have been broken over the years from lack of patience and kindness could be numbered in the thousands, and the heartaches from such cannot be measured! Due to many factors, very few couples are equal in all areas of life. If you as a wife are advanced in a certain area, it may be a temptation for you to become very impatient with your husband, but love will wait and help in every way possible, even to the point of discomfort. In fact, the King James Version uses "suffers long" for the word patience. Life is a growing process. A couple in love will grow together and patiently endure any short-comings of the other.

To rush some things in life will only destroy them. It is like the man who wanted his garden to grow faster than others, so he went out daily and stretched his plants. Later, to his surprise, he found them all dead. Be assured, love will wait.

Then, joined with patience is kindness. The apostle Paul's admonition to Christians in general certainly applies to husbands and wives: "and be ye kind one to another, tenderhearted, forgiving one another, even as God for Christ's sake hath forgiven you" (Ephesians 4:32). Usually, the impatient person is unkind. How about you, are you patient with your husband? Are you kind most of the time? How can a marriage be ideal and happy where unkindness is present? Some wives are kinder to a stranger than to their own husband. Remember the words of Solomon: "It is better to dwell in a corner of the house top, than with a brawling woman in a wide house" (Proverbs 21:9). Most husbands feel this way. Could this be why some husbands spend as much time as possible away from home or why they seek relationships with others?

When there is love, there will be words of kindness. This is not to say that all will be smooth sailing. Yes, there will be trying times in your marriage, but be assured where there is true love, kindness will prevail.

2. LOVE IS NOT JEALOUS, CONCEITED, OR PROUD.

The deeper the stream of love runs, the less jealousy there will be, because love generates trust. The only love in jealousy is self-love. The jealous heart always sees more than is there and views all circumstances through magnifying glasses. How can you say, "I love my husband" when filled with doubts caused by jealousy? Some who have no grounds for doubts are heard to say: "I'm jealous because I love." How wrong! Love builds trust, not jealousy. Jealousy is not the fruits of true love: "For jealousy is the rage of a man" (Proverbs

6:34a). "For love is strong as death; jealousy is cruel as the grave" (Song of Solomon 8:6). Someone has rightfully said: "The jealous man (woman) poisons his own banquet, and then eats it."

In an ideal marriage, jealousy is removed by love on the part of both husband and wife as each one works to remove doubts.

3. LOVE IS NOT ILL-MANNERED, SELFISH OR IRRITATED.

When a romance is blooming in courtship, most couples highly respect each other and go the extra mile to exalt the other, but in far too many cases, after marriage this is all forgotten. Especially is this true when love is not present. With the presence of love, however, the circumstances are different. The passing of years brings respect, and it never seems a waste of time to show courtesy.

One of the first symptoms of the lack of love is selfishness! Be assured, selfishness leaves destruction in its path. The selfish woman (or man) feels that her mate has nothing better to do in life than to please her! Marriages that are built on selfishness do not stand on firm ground. Those who love to the point that they are willing to lose themselves trying to make their partner happy will find true happiness and gain far more than they are able to give.

4. LOVE KEEPS NO RECORD OF WRONGS.

This is another way of saying that when there is love, there is forgiveness. All of us are human beings, subject to mistakes, and need forgiveness! "To err is human; to forgive, divine" (Pope). Love is the reason why divine forgiveness is offered in the Bible: (John 3:16; John 15:13).

In a marriage relationship, usually the one that refuses to forgive is the one that needs forgiveness most. Why is it easy for a mother to forgive her children? Because she loves them, and love forgives. If your husband goes wrong, and sincerely asks you to forgive, but you refuse, the precious ingredient of love is missing.

Love keeps no record of wrongs; when a wife forgives, she forgets. Too many times, mistakes are remembered and brought up often to harm him, but not so when there is love. A true illustration of forgiveness comes to us from God: "I, even I, am he that blotteth out thy transgressions for mine own sake, and will not remember thy sins" (Isaiah 43:25).

In an ideal marriage, bound by love, each day is a new beginning as each partner desires that all wrongs be forgiven and forgotten. And with the help of God, and forgiveness through his Son, the land of beginning in which the poet Tarkington dreamed can be found:

I wish there were some wonderful place
    Called the land of beginning again,
Where all our mistakes and all our heartaches
    And all our poor selfish grief
Could be dropped like a shabby old coat at the door
    And never put on again.

5. LOVE IS HAPPY WITH TRUTH— UNHAPPY WITH EVIL.

Love looks for the best in your husband while a lack of love searches out evil. Love "beareth all things, believeth all things, hopeth all things, endureth all things" (1 Corinthians 13:7). Love will help you find the good life and will work overtime to avoid evil. An ideal marriage, motivated by love, helps each partner overcome the pitfalls of evil.

Truth is positive and should be respected by all. Love will exalt truth and refuse to associate with evil. Think of the marriages that have failed because evil was entertained instead of truth.

Truly then, an ideal marriage must be based on the principle of love. The apostle Paul closes his list of principles by saying that love is eternal: "Love never faileth" (1 Corinthians 13:8a). God intended that marriage be based on love and that it endure even until death.

Love must be developed in marriage if the oneness that God intended is to be maintained. It takes two pulling together, and when this is done, love will grow. It will not be easy in many cases, but the reward will be happiness, because LOVE PAYS GREAT DIVIDENDS. Marriage is from God, and God is love — an ideal marriage will have love.

DISCUSSION QUESTIONS
THOU SHALT SEEK AN IDEAL MARRIAGE

1.   Define an "ideal marriage" built on love.

2. Discuss the many definitions for love from class members.

3. How is love recognized in the Bible?

4. What is meant by the statement: "An ideal marriage does not happen by chance".

5. Why is the virtue of patience so essential between husbands and wives?

6. Give some examples of unkind wives.

7. Why are some wives kinder to strangers than to their husbands?

8. Does jealousy have a place in love?

9. What will pride do to a marriage?

10. When love is not present, and respect lost, what happens between husbands and wives?

11. Discuss forgiveness with a love that keeps no records.

12. How important is it for wives to look for the best in their husbands?

13. Discuss the dividends paid by love.

HUSBANDS

1. Do you feel that most husbands really want an ideal marriage?

2. Does the husband's definition of love often differ from that of the wife?

3. What of the husband's statement: "I love you, but don't know how to show it?"

4. What of the husband's statement: "I love you, even though I don't get around to telling you."

5.   Give some examples of an unkind and impatient husband.

6.   Does Solomon's statement in Proverbs 21:9 apply to men as well as women? Discuss.

7.   Discuss the damage that can be done by a jealous husband.

8.   In what ways are husbands tempted to have pride in their marriages?

9.   Discuss ways in which husbands are often ill-mannered.

10.   On a scale of one to ten, how would you rate husbands in regard to being able to forgive?

11.   What happens when husbands hold grudges?

12.   How does Paul's statement: "Love never fails" apply to all facets of marriage?

IX

Thou Shalt Have The Right Attitude Toward Thy Husband

Chapter Nine

THOU SHALT HAVE THE RIGHT ATTITUDE TOWARD THY HUSBAND.

Here is another commandment for wives that is essential if a smooth and happy marriage is to be enjoyed. Be assured that you will have some type of attitude toward your husband because there is no way that you can drift along through life with no attitude. The attitude you have toward him will either be good or bad! A bad attitude will destroy faster than both of you can build up, while a good one will overlook a multitude of faults. There are two major ways that we display our attitude – by the way we talk, and by the way we act. Both of these are very important.

BY THE WAY WE TALK

How much respect do you show your husband in your daily conversation? Words that are cutting, destructive, and demanding won't accomplish anything good. In fact, day by day, they will build up to an explosion which will weaken your marriage. Many women storm out at their children, and then do the same to their husbands. If your husband ever feels that you are commanding him as a child, he will feel deprived of his role as husband, headship, and even manhood. This will harm seriously any relationship between you.

However, the opposite is true when a good attitude is displayed by proper words. It takes no more energy to make requests of love, and yet, the results are astronomical. Just a few choice words such as: "Honey, would you please help me?" Or, "Darling, could you please assist me?" Or "Honey, I would appreciate you carrying out the garbage", will do wonders. Yes, what we say and the tone we use when saying it, can help or harm a relationship.

BY THE WAY WE ACT

Some bite their tongues to make sure they say the right words to their husbands, and then display a terrible attitude by the way they act. Right words and right actions must be coupled together. The way we act has a language all of its own. The wife that is purposely banging things around in the kitchen, and talking only when asked direct questions is saying, "I'm upset". As she passes by her husband, she would not touch him for anything in the world. She may not be saying the wrong words, but her body language is saying volumes!

On the other hand, suppose she is quietly preparing a meal while humming a song, and joining in gladly in a conversation with her husband? Suppose as she crosses the kitchen she pats him on the shoulder or hurriedly plants a kiss on his cheek or lips, what is she saying by her actions? Needless to say, this is the kind of attitude a husband loves.

Since it is so important to keep a good attitude as a wife, what are some of the things one should avoid? Hopefully, the following will help:

1. DON'T POUT FOR LONG PERIODS OF TIME.

It would be needless to tell you not to ever pout! This is a thing that sooner or later overtakes everyone. There will be cutting words, disappointments, and heated arguments. After these moments, pouting may seem as natural as breathing. However, this type of pouting may be done without any real damage. The problem arises when pouting is extended over a long period of time.

What really happens when you are pouting? You have cut yourself off from conversation, happy feelings, and closeness with your husband. You don't want to talk with him, feed him, hold him, or love him. If the pouting is allowed to continue, you may not even desire to sleep with him in the same bed. You will not pout long before he decides to do the same, and several days and nights may pass in this miserable condition. This is to the husband, the fullest meaning of being in the "dog house". Some couples pout so long that they finally forget why they began pouting in the first place, but still feel rejection, coldness, and resentment toward each other. If practiced often, this can deteriorate a marriage relationship. Thus, both husband and wife need to avoid long periods of pouting.

One of the best antidotes for pouting is, "Honey, I'm sorry", or "please forgive me" along with some hugging and kissing.

2. DON'T EXPECT YOUR HUSBAND TO BE SOMEONE ELSE.

To help you keep a good attitude toward your husband, don't expect him to be someone else. There is certainly nothing wrong in a wife seeking to bring out the best in her husband, or in trying to help him overcome weaknesses! This is one of the privileges of being a good help meet (suitable help), provided she goes about such in the right way. Yet, she must never lose sight of the fact that he is a unique person. God has not made all men the same. Some love hunting and fishing, while others do not! Some love the land, planting and growing, while others do not. Even if you have the power to drive him from the things he loves, he will not be truly fulfilled and happy. Let him be himself!

You may observe another man that you feel serves as a perfect model that you desire your husband to be. On the surface you may see in him a great improvement over that of your husband. But if you really knew the weaknesses of this so-called model, your husband would be perhaps greater. Love your husband, then, for who he is, and don't try to make him into someone else. Any effort to make the change will display before your husband a destructive attitude.

3. DON'T FEEL YOU COULD NEVER LOSE YOUR HUSBAND

There are many ways a husband can be lost, and failing to realize this causes many wives to develop a destructive attitude. There are those wives (also husbands) who feel that once the marriage ceremony is over, I now have my husband hooked. During courtship she tried to do everything just right, and her attitude was almost without spot. However, believing that she has him for life, she may develop the "I don't care" attitude — and "now that I have him, I can't lose him". If you are guilty of this attitude, please be reminded of the various ways to lose a husband:

SEPARATION

There are some husbands that reach the point where they do not wish to live with their wives any longer, therefore, they desire separation. They may not have any grounds for divorce and remarriage, but they simply desire to live alone. There are many factors that may bring a man to this point, but basically there are two very important ones. First of all, he may have reached the point where his wife causes him to lose his self-respect. Whether or not he deserves this, the effect is still the same. Therefore, he chooses a separate life to get away from this problem. In the second place, she may have cut him off from all sexual union with her, and he reaches the point where he does not feel married and obligated to pretend. A separation may be a mutual agreement, as he continues support, or it may be a legal separation where his responsibilities are legally spelled out, but in either case, there is a separation.

DIVORCE

Even though this is a word that we (especially Christians) do not wish to consider, it is nevertheless too often present. In spite of the strictness of Bible teaching in regard to divorce, thousands are still caught up in it. Our nation as a whole is seeking divorces at record breaking speed, and the percent of divorces climbs higher each year. And who would deny that the problem of divorce has made inroads into Christianity? Remember, many of these felt at one time that they could never lose each other!

LOST AT HOME

An article written by Joe R. Barnett in *Upreach* Magazine begins: "Two people may withdraw from each other so completely that, in effect, divorce has taken place though they continue to live in the same house" (Vol. 4, No. 2, pp. 19).

It would be shocking to know how many wives or husbands have lost their mates even though they are still pretending and simply playing house. This does not appear to be all that serious on the surface, but to the couples living out the drama, it means unhappiness. Again, it would be frightening to know how many of these situations developed because of the wrong attitude.

It is a fact that marriages among Christian couples have a far greater chance of survival than of others, but how foolish it is to think that such will happen without effort. As we have just found, there is more than one way to lose your mate. Therefore, develop the right attitude toward your husband. Work on a daily basis to love and hold him. Don't make the mistake of waiting until he is lost to hold him – this can be too late!

When Robert Young, the famous actor known to millions as Dr. Marcus Welby, was asked why he and his wife had lived together fifty years, he quoted his wife's explanation: "I guess it's because we have done a lot of laughing and kissing together."

DISCUSSION QUESTIONS
THOU SHALT HAVE THE RIGHT ATTITUDE TOWARD THY HUSBAND

1. Analyze what is involved in attitudes.

2. Show how we display a good or bad attitude by the way we talk.

3. Show how we display a good or bad attitude by the way we act.

4. Discuss the positive and negative aspects of pouting.

5. How do a husband and wife break a spell of pouting?

6. To what extent can you change your husband, and to what extent must he not change?

7. How does the Proverb, "grass is greener on the other side of the fence" usually work out when comparing your husband to other men?

8. Discuss the dangers that arise when a husband or wife feels that they can never lose their mate?

9. Name and discuss two major causes of separation.

10. Compare separation and legal separation.

11. Discuss the problem of divorce in the church.

12. In what sense can divorce take place even though a couple continues to live in the same house?

13. Discuss some efforts that can be made to avoid divorce.

HUSBANDS

1. Do husbands respond more readily to being driven or led?

2. To what degree do husbands pout?

3. Why is the term "being in the dog house" applied to husbands instead of wives?

4. Are more husbands selfish in regard to their hunting, fishing, gardens, etc?

5. Discuss how a wife should deal with her husband's hobbies.

6. Is it possible for a wife to overlook good traits in her husband because of his weaker ones?

7. To what extent do husbands take their wives for granted because they don't feel that they could ever lose them?

8. How do you feel about a rejected husband desiring to live alone?

9. Why do husbands get divorces?

10. Discuss the value of laughing and kissing a lot in regard to holding a marriage together.

X

Thou Shalt Learn
To Communicate

Chapter Ten

THOU SHALT LEARN TO COMMUNICATE.

The tenth Commandment for wives is a very difficult command to obey, and yet so important. It is so common to hear wives say: "We just can't talk!" Or, "When we talk, we don't communicate." Perhaps at this point it would be helpful to consider why many husbands and wives do not communicate:

1. SOME WILL NOT TRY.

It is a fact that many couples simply refuse to talk. This is not to say that they do not engage in conversations, but rather, they do not talk about the issues that are tearing the marriage apart. It is important, if true communication is to be accomplished, that each be willing to talk. It is so easy to take the attitude, "I'll just ignore these problems and maybe they will go away." The truth of the matter is that they won't! In fact, they will compound themselves until they grow into an unsurmountable mountain. Therefore, the first step in seeking to communicate is to try.

2. SOME ARE TOO SELFISH.

There are couples tht are willing to try, but still fail because one or both are selfish. If you enter the conversation with the attitude that I know I'm right and he's wrong, you will never communicate properly. In your mind, you may feel that you are right, but it is always possible that you're not! Even if you are right, you should never close your mind to his side. It is important that a husband and wife, however, seek out the truth regardless of who is right or wrong.

3. SOME ARE TOO ARGUMENTATIVE.

Thousands of couples never achieve true communication because all attempts to do so simply become heated arguments. It would be impossible to embark upon a husband-wife conversation in regard to problems without emotions, but to accomplish anything, both must keep their emotions under control. Otherwise, any attempt to communicate will drive the wedge that divides them deeper.

When an attempt for communication is simply an argument, each will be playing a game and will be trying to win a point over the other. Consequently, harsh things will be said that drive out love, and more damage than good will result.

4. SOME WAIT TOO LONG.

It is likewise a fact that many couples fail in communication because they wait until the problem is totally out of hand before any effort is made to seriously talk about it. Once the feelings have been cut deeply, it is more difficult to heal the wounds. It is so easy to think, "we need to talk, but I'm so busy, maybe later." By the time many postponements take place, the problem has become more acute.

Therefore, we can see a few of the stumbling blocks in the paths of husbands and wives who are trying to communicate. Assuming we are able to remove these and other hindrances, how does a couple communicate? Please study carefully the following suggestions:

PLAN A TIME TO TALK.

To plan a time to talk is important because it reminds each party that this conversation is important. Too often such is not planned and efforts are made at the most inopportune times. One may want to talk, while the other is extremely busy, or carrying some heavy mental assignment, and all will fail. Be assured, it is important for both parties to be in the proper frame of mind to properly communicate.

When making plans, discuss a specific time and place. Some couples might like to have a dinner date and afterward talk. This is a great setting for communication, especially if you can sit at a table away from the crowd. In this setting, there will be less temptation to raise your voices in anger.

Still others might prefer talking at home while the children are away, or some might choose to go for a drive. Each couple can choose their own place, but the important point is to plan a place and time.

MAP OUT A PLAN.

Some couples try to talk out their problems without any type of plan. Consequently, they may find themselves talking in circles and finally getting into a heated argument. This is not to say that you should have a highly sophisticated, legal type plan, but rather a simple step by step procedure.

The first goal in such a plan is to define the problem, and this should certainly be done by both husband and wife. At the very beginning it may be learned that you do not understand the problem alike. However, if it is learned that you agree on the problem, you have a common ground to seek a solution.

TALK ABOUT POSSIBLE SOLUTIONS.

Usually there are certain obstacles within a marriage causing the problem. Before getting to these, first write down the things in which you agree. It is certainly best to begin with the areas where you agree. Next, discuss the general problems in your marriage. It may be such things as money, your children, your relatives or his, and employment problems. After these general problems have been discussed, it is time to get down to personal things. This will be the most difficult of all and therefore, should be handled with all the kindness and gentleness possible. When you are dealing with his problems, don't approach him with a "better-than-thou" attitude. This certainly applies also in his case. When this is done, the other will rebel and all doors of communication will be closed.

WRITE DOWN GRIEVANCES.

The next step in seeking a solution to your personal problems is for each to write down three or four grievances against the other. Remember, this is to be done, not to criticize, but to help. If such becomes a way of putting the other down, or getting even for hurts of the past, all will fail. Once these are written down, you should take turns discussing number one. For example, once you have discussed his number one grievance, then you should consider your number one grievance against him. After you have completed both lists, if all has been discussed in the proper way, you should both feel closer to each other and willing to try harder in the future for a richer relationship.

TALK TOGETHER OFTEN.

All of your problems will not be solved with one attempt. This initial effort is merely a foundation on which you can build in the future. True communication will produce a change, but it will be necessary to talk together often. When you see failures in a certain area, simply say, "We need to talk." When you get back together to talk, you will want to refer to the plans that were originally made, and if both are willing to try, there should be total forgiveness for any failures. This is certainly not the place for ridicule or severe criticism.

Please remember also, that further talk is necessary even if the problems are resolved. Why not talk together of your success? Let him know if you are now happy and that you appreciate his effort, and you will need the same assurance from him. Use every opportunity to reinforce the need for communication. You may make such statements as: "I'm glad we talked," "let's never cut each other off again," or "when we have a problem in the future, let's talk."

Finally, don't wait too late to talk or communicate. It is a fact that too many couples seek to communicate after their marriage is on the rocks. How difficult it is to truly communicate after hatred is built up. Remember, poor communication between husbands and wives blocks the flow of love.

DISCUSSION QUESTIONS
THOU SHALT LEARN TO COMMUNICATE

1. How serious is it when husbands and wives can't talk?

2. Discuss why it is so important for both parties to be willing to talk.

3. Why does selfishness kill all communication?

4. What is the difference between arguing and talking?

5. Discuss the dangers of husbands and wives waiting too long before attempting communication.

6. What are the advantages of planning a time to talk?

7. Where do you feel is the most appropriate place for a husband and wife to talk?

8. What is involved in defining the problem to be discussed between a couple?

9. Discuss some of the obstacles that cause problems in marriage.

10. Talk about the danger of husband or wife having the "better-than-thou" attitude.

11. What is the advantage of fairly listing and discussing each one's grievances?

12. When one or both fail after communication, what should be the proper attitude?

HUSBANDS

1. Why is it difficult for many husbands to talk to their wives about marital problems?

2. Are husbands more apt to "put off" communication hoping things will be alright?

3. To what extent does selfishness affect husbands?

4. Should the wife wait for the husband to plan a time for communication?

5. What usually happens when problems are discussed without a plan?

6. Why is it important to communicate often?

7. To what extent should husbands display love while talking to their wives?

8. Discuss some of the areas hardest to talk about with your wife.

BACKGROUND MATERIAL

SEX AND THE BIBLE

INTRODUCTION

The story is told of a huge tree in Colorado which stood for four hundred years. During that time it was struck by lightning fourteen times and stood against innumerable avalanches and storms, yet it continued to survive. Do you know what finally destroyed it? Beetles! Yes, beetles destroyed the inner part of the giant tree and ended its life.

As we look back over the history of America, we can be proud of her many victories and her strength. Enemies have come against her, but to no avail! However, just like the great tree, the greatest threat to America is not from without, but from within. All the stock piles of bombs and military forces will not stop this enemy. Like the beetles that destroyed the huge tree, low morals are eating away at our great God-founded country, and they had their base in the sexual revolution. Truly, the so called "new morality" has replaced the pure and high standards of the Bible in the lives of millions! Instead of being led by the word of God, too many are being led by the philosophy of "anything goes, do as you please", or "eat, drink and be merry for tomorrow we die."

This kind of living can be expected of those of the world, but thousands who claim to be Christians have also boarded the band wagon and are ignoring God's will. We beg of you to stop for a few minutes and think! Let your minds perceive what God has taught in His book, the Bible. We cannot afford to drift any longer with the tide of the world. The apostle John wrote: "Love not the world, neither the things that are in the world. If any man love the world, the love of the Father is not in him" (1 John 2:15).

1. GOD'S ORIGINAL PLAN.

In studying what the Bible says about sex, it is appropriate to begin with Genesis 2:18 where, after making man, God said: "It is not good that the man should be alone; I will make him an help meet for him". Therefore, God made Eve, brought her unto Adam, and said: "Therefore shall a man leave his father and his mother, and shall cleave unto his wife: and they shall be one flesh" (Genesis 2:23-24). Later, in Genesis 4:1, we are told: "And Adam knew Eve his wife; and she conceived, and bare Cain, and said, I have gotten a man from the Lord." Thus, we can see that God placed the sexual relationship in marriage; however, the Bible reveals that it did not remain there. By the time of the flood in Noah's time: "God saw that the wickedness of man was great in the earth, and that every imagination of the thoughts of his heart was only evil continually" (Genesis 6:5). Again, "And God looked upon the earth, and, behold, it was corrupt; for all flesh had corrupted his way upon the earth" (Genesis 6:12).

The great flood cleansed the earth of the wickedness of man, but the years following found him once again drifting from God and His divine plan. Always included in man's long list of sins were adultery and fornication.

2. ADULTERY AND FORNICATION.

The word "adultery" is found throughout the pages of the Old and New Testaments. It is translated from the Greek word "moikeia", which means "to have unlawful intercourse with another man's wife, to commit adultery with" (Thayer's Greek English Lexicon). How did God feel about this corruption? Under the Law of Moses, one of the ten commandments stated: "Thou shalt not commit adultery" (Exodus 20:14). The penalty for adultery was death! "If a man be found lying with a woman married to a husband, then they shall both of them die, both the man that lay with the woman, and the woman: so shalt thou put away evil from Israel" (Deuteronomy 22:22). Many of the wise sayings of the Book of Proverbs also warn against adultery: "But whoso committeth adultery with a woman lacketh understanding: he that doeth it destroyeth his own soul" (Proverbs 6:32).

When we come to the New Testament, in addition to the word "adultery," the word "fornication" is used. This word is from the Greek "porneia", which means: "illicit sexual intercourse in general" (Thayer's Greek English Lexicon). Thus, fornication includes adultery, but goes further to include ALL illicit sexual activity, including the illicit sexual relations of the unmarried as well as the homosexual.

Other than death the only exception Jesus gives for remarriage is fornication: "And I say unto you, Whosoever shall put away his wife, except it be for fornication, and shall marry another, committeth adultery: and whoso marrieth her which is put away doth commit adultery" (Matthew 19:9). No wonder the apostle Paul warned: "Flee fornicaiton. Every sin that a man doeth is without the body; but he that committeth fornication sinneth against his own body" (1 Corinthians 6:18). He had just previously written: "Now the body is not for fornication, but for the Lord; and the Lord for the body" (1 Corinthians 6:13b). In the Thessalonian letter, Paul further stated: "For this is the will of God, even your sanctification, that ye should abstain from fornication: That every one of you should know how to possess his vessel in sanctification and honour" (1 Thessalonians 4:3-4).

How can anyone claim to be a Christian and engage in these practices of the devil? When Paul listed some of the works of the flesh, he names as the first two, adultery and fornication. After naming some 17 lustful works, including such evils as murderers and drunkenness, he concluded: "that they which do such things shall not inherit the kingdom of God" (Colossians 3:5). Then, to the Roman Christians, he asked: "How shall we, that are dead to sin, live any longer therein?" (Romans 6:2).

3. HOMOSEXUALITY AND LESBIANISM.

Many Bible students can see the similarities between the cities of Sodom and Gomorrah and America today. The history of Sodom and Gomorrah is found in Genesis 18 and 19. Three men, representing God, visited Abraham to announce the birth of Isaac. After this was accomplished, they turned their attention toward the cities of Sodom and Gomorrah because the sins of the people there were very grievous. At this point, Abraham made intercession to save the cities; he pled: "If there be fifty righteous found will you spare the city?" The Lord said he would, but fifty could not be found. Thus

Abraham continued his request for forty-five, forty, thirty, twenty, and finally only ten! Again the Lord agreed to save the city for the sake of ten righteous people, but not even ten could be found (Genesis 18:32). Therefore, the verdict was that these cities must be destroyed!

Now, what was the nature of their wickedness? Were they murderers, liars, thieves? Perhaps so, but such are not mentioned. According to Genesis 19, the men of the city were homosexuals. Lot, the nephew of Abraham, lived in Sodom with his family. When the Lord determined to destroy these cities he sent two angeis, in the form of men, to visit Lot. Lot insisted that they spend the night and they accepted. Notice the reactions of the men of the city: "But before they lay down, the men of the city, even the men of Sodom, compassed the house round, both old and young, all the people from every quarter: and they called unto Lot, and said unto him, where are the men which came in to thee this night? Bring them out unto us, that we may know them. And Lot went out at the door unto them, and shut the door after him. And said,"I pray you, brethren, do not so wickedly" (Genesis 19:4-7). But Lot could not dissuade them. He even offered them his two daughters, but they refused saying: "Stand back!" "And they pressed sore upon the man, even Lot, and came near to break the door" (v. 9). The angels pulled Lot back into the house: "and smote the men that were at the door of the house with blindness, both small and great: so that they wearied themselves to find the door" (v. 11).

After Lot, his wife and two daughters were ushered out of the city, we read: "Then the Lord rained upon Sodom and upon Gomorrah brimstone and fire from the Lord out of heaven" (Genesis 19:25).

Now, in view of this Old Testament example, have the days of Sodom and Gomorrah returned today? We have only to keep up with the current events to know that this issue is alive and moving forward. There are those that want this sin of Sodom made legal and respectable. The battle is not limited to men, but women (Lesbians) are also engaged in the fight. The God-given idea of marriage, the home, and sexual relations between husband and wives are being mocked with efforts to destroy.

4. HOMOSEXUALITY IS FORNICATION.

As we have already learned, the Greek word for fornication is "porneia". This is the root of pornography and includes homosexual activities as well as all other illicit sexual actions. But how do we know that the men of Sodom and Gomorrah, as homosexuals, committed fornication? In the Book of Jude verse 7 we find: "Even as Sodom and Gomorrah and the cities about them in like manner, giving themselves over to fornication, and going after strange flesh, are set forth for an example, suffering the vengeance of eternal fire." Please notice that they gave themselves over to fornication.

When we turn to the writings of Paul in Romans 1, we read about the depraved condition of the heathen world in the first century and our minds are drawn to the evil of the twentieth century. He begins by saying: "For the wrath of God is revealed from heaven against all ungodliness and unrighteousness..." (v. 18). Then he continues by listing their sins. First he speaks of their image worship and then of their corrupted morals: "Wherefore God also gave them up to uncleanness through the lusts of their own hearts, to dishonour their own bodies between themselves" (v. 24). "For this cause God gave them up unto vile affections: for even their women did change the natural use into that which is against nature" (v. 26). This is the sin of Lesbianism) Next Paul turns to the men: "And likewise also the men, leaving the natural use of the woman, burned in their lust one toward another: men with men working that which is unseemly...." (v. 27). This is the sin of homosexuality! When Paul summed up the consequences of these sins he wrote: "Who knowing the judgment of God, that they which commit such things are worthy of death, not only do the same, but have pleasure in them that do them" (Romans 1:32).

It is plain to see that Paul, guided by the Holy Spirit, condemns such sins. Christ had promised His apostles the Holy Spirit to guide them into all truth: "Howbeit when he, the Spirit of truth, is come, he will guide you into all truth" (John 16:13a). Therefore, when Paul condemns the sin of homosexuality and Lesbianism, he is speaking truth for Jesus Christ. How can anyone uphold such practices and still claim to follow the Bible?

5. SEX AND MARRIAGE.

The same Bible that condemns adultery and fornication, highly approves of sex in marriage: "Let marriage be had in honor among all, and let the bed be undefiled: for fornicators and adulterers God will judge" (Hebrews 13:4). The apostle Paul gave his stamp of approval when he wrote to the Corinthians: "Nevertheless, to avoid fornication let every man have his own wife, and let every woman have her own husband" (1 Corinthians 7:1,2). Again he added: "But if they cannot contain, let them marry: for it is better to marry than to burn" (1 Corinthians 7:9). He even encouraged husbands and wives to fulfill the sexual needs of each other: "Let the husband render unto the wife due benevolence: and likewise also the wife unto the husband. The wife hath not power of her own body, but the husband: and likewise also the husband hath not power of his own body, but the wife. Defraud ye not one the other, except it be with consent for a time, that ye may give yourselves to fasting and prayer; and come together again, that Satan tempt you not for your incontinency" (1 Corinthians 7:3-5). Sexual relations outside of marriage are sinful! Within the Biblical marital relationship, we have God's approval, but outside, His condemnation. Man can ignore, pervert, and abuse God's word, but it still remains the truth.

6. STAND UP AND BE COUNTED.

The story is told of an elderly lady during the Civil War who looked out her window and saw enemy soldiers approaching. She ran immediately to the kitchen and got her broom. Her loved ones said,"Grandma, don't you know you can't win over all those soldiers with a broom?" With sparkling eyes she replied, "Yes, I know that, but when I'm finished, they'll know whose side I'm on!"

How about you? Does the world know whose side you are on? Have you stood up to be counted for the Lord? Only ten righteous people could have saved Sodom and Gomorrah from fire and brimstone. Are you represented as one of the ten?

GOD'S BLUEPRINT FOR THE HOME

In Genesis 6:14-22 where God commanded Noah to build an ark, He gave him a blueprint specifying the size, shape, stories, number of doors and windows, and even the kind of wood to be used. Noah was well pleasing to God because; "according to all that God commanded him, so did he." (Genesis 6:22).

After the children of Israel had been led safely out of Egyptian bondage, God not only gave them a written law, but also commanded that a tabernacle be constructed. God gave the pattern or blueprint of every detail from the large outer enclosure to the smallest furnishing. The writer of the book of Hebrews in the new

Testament later recorded God's admonition to Moses: "See, saith he, that thou make all things according to the pattern that was showed thee in the mount." (Hebrews 8:5).

Now, the same God that gave a blueprint for the ark and the tabernacle also gave one for the home. Just as surely as Noah and Moses could not please God without following the blueprint, neither can we please Him today without building our homes by His blueprint. Would you please take a close look at God's Blueprint of the Home.

1. DIVINE IN ORIGIN

Be assured that the home is not an invention of man, but comes from God! After God had made Adam, He saw that man was lonely. In Genesis 2:19,20, God brought the fowl and animals He had formed to Adam for naming. After naming them, Adam was still in need of a help meet, so God formed woman. When they were brought together, God laid down His law for marriage and the home: "Therefore shall a man leave his father and his mother, and shall cleave unto his wife: and they shall be one flesh," (Genesis 2:24). Later when Jesus quoted this original law from the Old Testament, he added: "What therefore God hath joined together, let not man put asunder." (Matthew 19:6).

The question is often asked today, "Why are so many marriages failing?" Many reasons can be given, but lying at the root of all is the fact that many do not really consider marriage divine. Most of us have seen marriages survive every storm of life because those involved believed the home is divine in origin.

Since marriage is divine, be assured that it is honorable. Some homes are broken because one or both partners feel guilty about the marital relationship. But do you think God would be the author of anything sinful? The Bible gives full approval of the home and marriage. It is the infidelity and other sins that are condemned, not marriage.

In Hebrews 13:4 we read: "Let marriage be had in honor among all, and let the bed be undefiled: for fornicators and adulterers God will judge." In fact, Solomon expresses God's feelings in these words: "Whoso findeth a wife findeth a good thing, and obtaineth favor of the Lord." (Proverbs 18:22). Therefore, marriage that is kept within God's divine plan pleases Him. The only guilt that should be felt is when you as a husband or wife fail to carry out your God given responsibility as a marriage partner.

God's plan for marriage is not compulsory if one can refrain from fornication! During the times of heavy persecution in the New Testament age, Paul even advised: "It is good for a man not to touch a woman". But then he continues: "Nevertheless, to avoid fornication, let every man have his own wife, and let every woman have her own husband." (1 Corinthians 7:1,2). Again he advises: "But if they cannot contain, let them marry: for it is better to marry than to burn." (1 Corinthians 7:9).

2. UNITED IN CONSTRUCTION

In God's blueprint for the home, He intended that man and woman be united in construction. From the moment that God brought woman to man, Adam said: "This is now bone of my bones, and flesh of my flesh: she shall be called Woman, because she was taken out of Man." (Genesis 2:23). In the very next verse God adds: "and they shall be one flesh." Surely the idea of "one flesh" involves the sexual union, but must not begin and end with this! In fact, the apostle Paul compares the oneness of husband and wife to the oneness of Christ and His church: "For the husband is the head of the wife, even as Christ is the head of the church: and he is the saviour of the body". (Ephesians 5:23). Paul continues in verse 24 by saying: "Therefore as the church is subject unto Christ so let the wives be to their own husbands in every thing. Husbands, love your wives, even as Christ also loved the church, and gave himself for it." To further show the oneness in construction of husbands and wives, Paul continues: "So ought men to love their wives as their own bodies. He that loveth his wife loveth himself. For no man ever yet hated his own flesh; but nourisheth and cherisheth it, even as the Lord the church" (Ephesians 5:28,29).

3. PROCREATIVE IN DESIGN

One of the first things God said to man and woman is recorded in Genesis 1:28: "Be fruitful and multiply and replenish the earth and subdue it." Having children and rearing them for the Lord are spiritual privileges. Children that are brought into this world and trained in the "nurture and admonition of the Lord" become our greatest joy.

But we often hear people say: "I refuse to have a family because the world is too wicked!" Who would deny that the world is truly in a sinful condition, but is it not a fact that this has always been the case? God destroyed the whole human race, except for eight souls, during Noah's day because of wickedness. He also destroyed the cities of Sodom and Gomorrah because ten righteous people could not be found! But in a wicked world, God wants us to rear children for Him.

In the New Testament age (a very wicked age influenced by Roman corruption) Paul wrote to Timothy: "I desire therefore that the younger widows marry, bear children, rule the household...." (1 Timothy 5:14). God wants parents and children to refuse the ways of the world and follow His will. "Children, obey your parents in the Lord for this is right. Honor thy father and mother (which is the first commandment with promise) that it may be well with thee, and thou mayest live long on the earth." (Ephesians 6:1-3). Then Paul continues with this admonition to fathers: "And, ye fathers, provoke not your children to wrath: but nurture them in the chastening and admonition of the Lord." (Verse 4).

Yes, the idea of parenthood and rearing children can become a disappointment if God's blueprint is not followed, but when followed faithfully, procreation between husband and wife can be one of the finest blessings of the home.

4. MUTUAL IN OBLIGATION

Most of my life I have heard that marriage is a 50-50 proposition, but now I disagree with this! A successful marriage is a 100-100 proposition! Both the husband and wife must give 100 per cent; each must give all. After God made Adam He said: "It is not good that the man should be alone; I will make him an help meet for him." (Genesis 2:18). Some think the Bible says "help mate" but no, it says "help meet"! The word "meet" means suitable - thus, "help suitable". Man and woman must complement each other, and when each follows his or her God-given responsibility, this will be true. Each will stand up for the other! The children in home will never be allowed to speak disrespectfully against parent without the other correcting them. A father is not much of a man if he allows his children to speak against their mother. The same principle applies also to the mother!

The husband and wife will be mutually in love. Someone has said: "The most important thing a father can do for his children is to love their mother." How true is this statement! All couples should follow the principles of 1 Corinthians 13, the love chapter. If they do, notice what they will follow: "Love is very patient, very kind; Love knows no jealousy; Love makes no parade, Gives itself no airs, is never rude, never selfish; Never irritated, never resentful, Love is never glad, when others go wrong. Love is gladdened by goodness, Always slow to expose, Always eager to believe the best, Always hopeful, always patient; Love never disappears." Think of how many homes would be saved if such were followed!

God also intended that there be mutual sexual gratification between husband and wife. When either neglects the other, God's will is violated and the chances of a broken home are greater. The apostle Paul — guided by the Holy Spirit — gives this responsibility in few words: "Let the husband render unto the wife her due: and likewise also the wife unto the husband. The wife hath not power over her own body, but the husband: and likewise also husband hath not power over his own body, but the wife. Defraud ye not one another, except it be by consent for a season, that ye may give yourselves unto prayer, and may be together again, that Satan tempt you not because of your incontinency." (1 Corinthians 7:3-5).

God wants this relationship kept within marriage and thus encourages the husband and wife to help each other in avoiding temptation. Failure at this point has broken up many homes.

5. INDISSOLUBLE IN NATURE

In God's original blueprint for the home, He did not include divorce, or putting away. Jesus quoted God's rule in Matthew 19:6: "What therefore God hath joined together, let not man put asunder." Then Jesus was asked about Moses allowing divorce in the Old Testament, but Jesus reminded them that this was done because of hard hearts and then adds: "but from the beginning it hath not been so." (verse 8). When you search the Bible from beginning to end, you will find only two reasons to unbind a marriage and both of these originated from sin. The first is death! Death was brought upon the human race because of sin. After Adam and Eve sinned, they were banned from the beautiful garden of Eden: "lest he put forth his hand, and take also of the tree of life, and eat, and live for ever" (Genesis 3:22). Thus, this became one of the ways to unbind marriage.

This is discussed by Paul in Romans 7:2-3: "For the woman which hath an husband is bound by the law to her husband so long as he liveth; but if the husband be dead, she is loosed from the law of her husband." He goes on in the next verse and says that if her husband be dead and she marries another that she will not be called an adulteress.

The second reason to unbind a marriage is taught by Christ. It is also brought about by sin. He puts it into simple words: "Whosoever shall put away his wife, except it be for fornication, and shall marry another, committeth adultery: and whoso marrieth her which is put away doth commit adultery." (Matthew 19:9). Of all the reasons, Jesus gives only one — fornication, which is adultery! Now, we may wish for other reasons, but death and adultery are the only two mentioned! And please remember, these are exceptions; God has always hated putting away. His will is: "let not man put asunder."

6. RELIGIOUS IN SPIRIT

This final portion of God's blueprint is very important. What was the first marriage problem? Removing faithfulness to God! Until Adam and Eve disobeyed God, they had a home too beautiful to imagine, but after this Adam had to till the ground by the sweat of his face, Eve had pain in childbirth, and even one of their sons, Cain, murdered his own brother, Abel. The most important question should be: "Does Jesus live in your home?" Whether or not your home is armed with the "sword of the Spirit, which is the Word of God" is vitally important.

A few years ago the FBI reported that homes in America have 90 million weapons — 35 million rifles, 30 million shotguns, and 24 million hand guns. In fact all of our armed forces combined have only five million. Now, there is nothing wrong with having guns, provided they are used properly, but it seems that being armed with the Bible and living by it are far more important!

Through all circumstances of life, from beginning to end, a home needs Christ. Someone has put it in these words:
Christ at the marriage altar.
Christ on the bridal journey.
Christ when the new home is set up.
Christ when the baby comes.
Christ when the baby dies.
Christ in the pinching times.
Christ in days of plenty.
Christ when the wedded pair walk toward the sunset gates.
Christ for time; Christ for eternity.
This is the secret of home.

Both parents need to be sincerely religious and faithfully following the word of God. There is not room for hypocrites in any home following God's blueprint! A truly happy home is found when it can be truthfully said in the words of Joshua: "As for me and my house, we will serve the Lord!"

Note:

Other Useful Books From Quality

Precious in the Sight of God
Lea Fowler

Meet My Friend David
Jane McWhorter

Decisions, Volume 1 and 2
Sherlie Rowe

Today's Victorious Woman, Volume 1 and 2
Mrs. J.B. Livingston

The Wise Woman Knows
Bessie Patterson

Science Bulletin Boards
John Hudson Tiner

Rising Above Strife
Nancy Inez Witte

Balance: A Modern Christian Challenge
Anna M. Griffith

Order from Quality Publications

or   your favorite bookstore.